WHAT IF YOU HAD AN
Animal Nose!?

by Sandra Markle

Illustrated by
Howard McWilliam

Scholastic Inc.

For Susan Johnson
and the students
of Hammett Bowen
Elementary School
in Ocala, Florida

Text copyright © 2017 by Sandra Markle
Illustrations copyright © 2017 by Howard McWilliam

ISBN 978-0-545-85922-6

20 19   21 22

Printed in the U.S.A.   40
First edition, January 2017

Book design by Kay Petronio

What if one day when you woke up and looked in the mirror, the nose on your face wasn't yours? What if, overnight, a wild animal's nose took its place?

TAPIR

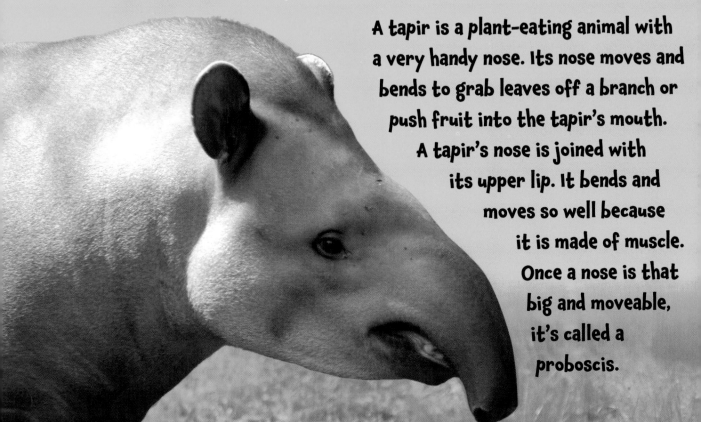

A tapir is a plant-eating animal with a very handy nose. Its nose moves and bends to grab leaves off a branch or push fruit into the tapir's mouth. A tapir's nose is joined with its upper lip. It bends and moves so well because it is made of muscle. Once a nose is that big and moveable, it's called a proboscis.

FACT

Tapirs mainly eat at night, so they bend their noses in all directions to sniff out food in the dark.

If you had a tapir's snout, you could catch a home-run ball, even with your hands full.

COTTONTAIL RABBIT

A rabbit's nose is packed with smell sensors. And rabbit noses twitch for many different reasons. A rabbit wiggles its nose up and down to pull more air in when it sniffs. That helps it find food or tell when hungry hunters are close so it can hop to safety. A rabbit's nose twitches faster when it is interested or excited—sometimes as many as 120 times a minute!

FACT

Rabbits have long, super-sensitive whiskers on either side of their nose. These whiskers help rabbits feel if a space is big enough to squeeze through—even in the dark!

If you had
a rabbit's nose,
your twitching nose
would show your
school spirit!

ELEPHANT

An elephant's nose may be the most useful nose on the planet. It's so long and special it even has its own name: a trunk. An elephant's trunk can sniff smells from lots of directions, even from up high. It can lift and carry something as heavy as a big log. An elephant also uses its trunk to pull in water—as much as two gallons at a time. Then it sprays a drink in its mouth or gives itself a shower.

FACT

The tip of an elephant's trunk works like fingers. It can pick up something as little as a peanut and pop it into its mouth.

If you had
an elephant's trunk,
you wouldn't need
to go to a water park
in the summer.

GRIZZLY BEAR

A grizzly bear's nose is packed with smell sensors. No wonder this bear is a champ at tracking down food—sometimes from over a mile away. It needs to find and eat all the food it can before winter. That's when a grizzly bear goes into a deep sleep called hibernation and usually doesn't eat at all.

FACT

The smell-sensing areas in a grizzly bear's nose are a hundred times bigger than a human's.

If you had a grizzly bear's nose, you could sniff out all your favorite goodies and only trick-or-treat at the best houses!

11

WARTHOG

A warthog's nose isn't pretty, but it's the perfect food finder. First the warthog uses its strong sense of smell to sniff out the underground roots and bulbs it likes to eat. Then the warthog rolls its nose around to dig into soft soil, with some help from its tusks. Finally, the warthog uses its nose to lift dirt out of the hole until it finds the roots or bulbs to munch.

FACT

Warthogs greet each other with nose-to-nose bumps.

If you had
a warthog's nose, you
would never need anything
but your nose to build
sand castles.

SAIGA

A saiga is a sheep-sized antelope with a proboscis nose. Its proboscis is lined with hairs and snotty mucus, making it perfect for filtering out dust. That's important because the saiga's homeland is often dry and dusty. Herds of saigas live together and kick up a lot of dust traveling in search of grass to eat.

FACT

Some saigas live in parts of Russia where winters are very cold. The saiga's big nose heats up icy air as the saiga breathes in.

If you had
a saiga's nose,
you would never
notice when a room
was dusty.

STAR-NOSED
MOLE

A star-nosed mole is a small, burrowing animal that uses its nose to find dinner in the dark underground—and sometimes even underwater. The star-nosed mole uses its nose to smell, but it also uses it to feel for food. Its nose has twenty-two fleshy rays around the nostrils. These are always moving. And, quick as a blink, the mole knows if its nose touches food, like a worm or an insect.

FACT

To smell underwater, the star-nosed mole blows bubbles and then sniffs, pulling the air bubbles into its nose, past its smell sensors.

If you had a star-nosed mole's nose, you could find a midnight snack without turning on the kitchen light.

17

RHINOCEROS

A rhinoceros is the only animal with a horn on its nose. It's made up of layers of keratin, the same stuff that human hair and fingernails are made of. Male rhinos use their horns to duel for mates. Females use theirs to guard their babies. Besides having a horn, a rhino's nose has a keen sense of smell to find leaves and fruit to eat. They can also sniff for enemies like lions.

FACT

A baby rhinoceros isn't born with a horn, but one soon starts growing and never stops.

If you had
a rhinoceros's nose,
you'd be the perfect
bodyguard.

19

GIANT
ANTEATER

What looks like a giant anteater's long nose is really its upper and lower jaws joined together. Its nose is on the tip of this long tube. This nose is perfect for poking into hard-to-reach places to sniff out yummy insects like ants and termites. A giant anteater also uses its long nose like a snorkel when it goes swimming so it can breathe while underwater.

FACT

When it smells insects, the giant anteater flicks its super-long tongue in and out quickly—as many as 160 times in a minute—and eats bugs by the thousands.

If you had a giant anteater's nose, you could go scuba diving without a snorkel.

21

BOURRET'S HORSESHOE BAT

A Bourret's horseshoe bat's nose makes it a super nighttime bug-hunter. Like other bats, a Bourret's horseshoe bat hunts by snorting high-pitched noises out its nose and listening for echoes of anything around them. But most bats shoot sounds in every direction at once. The shape of this bat's nose channels the sound so it can pinpoint exactly where to snag an insect.

FACT

To save energy, a Bourret's horseshoe bat often hangs from a branch while snorting noises. When an echo signals an insect is nearby, the bat flies after it.

If you had a Bourret's horseshoe bat's nose, you'd catch every fly that tried to spoil your picnic.

HAMMERHEAD SHARK

A hammerhead shark's nose is only for smelling—not breathing. The shark swings its head side to side, forcing water into a nostril near each eye. Because its nostrils are so far apart, the shark can tell if a fishy scent is stronger to the left or right. Then it tracks down its dinner.

FACT

A hammerhead shark can smell blood from wounded prey as far as a half mile away.

If you had a hammerhead shark's nose, you would always know the best places to fish.

25

A wild animal's nose could be cool for a while. But you don't use your nose to spray water or to dig in the ground. You don't need your nose to catch flies or to be a snorkel while you swim underwater.

And you'll never grab anything with your nose—no matter what. So if you could keep a wild animal nose for more than a day, what kind would be right for you?

Luckily, you don't have to choose. The nose on your face will always be a people nose.

It will be what you need to breathe and sniff all the scents around you. It's the perfect place to rest glasses if you need them to see better. Best of all, your nose is just what you need to look like you.

WHAT DOES YOUR NOSE DO FOR YOU?

Your nose starts with nostrils—twin openings for air to move in and out. Inside are passages lined with hairs and coated with mucus (snot). Together, these catch dust, germs, and pollen from plants that could bother your lungs—or even make you sick. Then you sneeze or blow out what your nose catches. Meanwhile, the air you breathe in also becomes warmer and wetter.

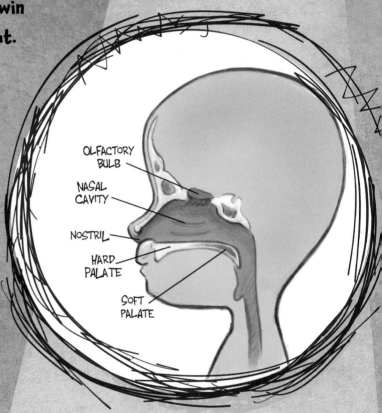

OLFACTORY BULB

NASAL CAVITY

NOSTRIL

HARD PALATE

SOFT PALATE

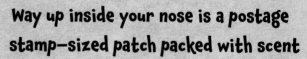

Way up inside your nose is a postage stamp–sized patch packed with scent sensors. These send signals to your brain, which let you know what you are smelling. At the same time, air travels down your throat to your windpipe and lungs. So your nose is the main way for you to get the air you need to live as well as to smell the world around you.

YOUR NOSE NEEDS YOU

For your nose's sake, you need to be careful what you breathe in. Stay away from cigarette smoke, and try not to breathe in fumes from harsh chemicals. If you live in a place where it gets cold, cover your nose with a scarf to shield it from chilly air. If you live where the air is very dry, place a humidifier in your home. That will make the air you breathe moister, which helps to prevent nosebleeds and colds. And if your nose feels clogged, blow gently.